budgetbooks

MOVIE THEMES

T0195136

ISBN 978-1-5400-4625-3

Visit Hal Leonard Online at
www.halleonard.com

Contact us:
Hal Leonard
7777 West Bluemound Road
Milwaukee, WI 53213
Email: info@halleonard.com

In Europe, contact:
Hal Leonard Europe Limited
42 Wigmore Street
Marylebone, London, W1U 2RN
Email: info@halleonardeurope.com

In Australia, contact:
Hal Leonard Australia Pty. Ltd.
4 Lentara Court
Cheltenham, Victoria, 3192 Australia
Email: info@halleonard.com.au

CONTENTS

AIRPORT LOVE THEME
(Winds of Chance)
from AIRPORT

Words by PAUL FRANCIS WEBSTER
Music by ALFRED NEWMAN

Slowly, with expression

ALL SYSTEMS GO

from APOLLO 13

Composed by
JAMES HORNER

LA VALSE D'AMELIE
from AMELIE

By YANN TIERSEN

13

AMERICAN BEAUTY
from the Dreamworks Major Motion Picture AMERICAN BEAUTY

By THOMAS NEWMAN

THE SEDUCTION
(Love Theme)
from the Paramount Motion Picture AMERICAN GIGOLO

Music by GIORGIO MORODER

DREAMS TO DREAM
(Finale Version)
from the Universal Motion Picture AN AMERICAN TAIL: FIEVEL GOES WEST

Words and Music by JAMES HORNER
and WILL JENNINGS

Slightly faster

THE CIDER HOUSE RULES

(Main Titles)

from the Miramax Motion Picture THE CIDER HOUSE RULES

By RACHEL PORTMAN

23

cresc.

GEORGE VALENTIN
from the Motion Picture THE ARTIST

Composed by LUDOVIC BOURCE

To Coda ⊕

WALTZ FOR PEPPY
from the Motion Picture THE ARTIST

Composed by LUDOVIC BOURCE

PROLOGUE & PROLOGUE PT. 2

from BEAUTY AND THE BEAST

Music by ALAN MENKEN

PROLOGUE PT. 2
Music by ALAN MENKEN
and CHRISTOPHER BENSTEAD

Moderately, in 2

WALLACE COURTS MURRON
from the Motion Picture BRAVEHEART

Music by JAMES HORNER

45

BREAKFAST AT TIFFANY'S

Theme from the Paramount Picture BREAKFAST AT TIFFANY'S

Music by HENRY MANCINI

BRIAN'S SONG
Theme from the Screen Gems Television Production BRIAN'S SONG

Music by MICHEL LEGRAND

Moderately, expressively

THE WINGS
from BROKEBACK MOUNTAIN

By GUSTAVO SANTAOLALLA

CHOCOLAT
(Main Titles)
from the Motion Picture CHOCOLAT

By RACHEL PORTMAN

Moderately, in 2

STORYBOOK
from CHRISTOPHER ROBIN

Music by GEOFF ZANELLI

A NARNIA LULLABY

from THE CHRONICLES OF NARNIA: THE LION, THE WITCH AND THE WARDROBE

Music by
HARRY GREGSON-WILLIAMS

1

COUSINS
(Love Theme)
from the Paramount Picture COUSINS

Music by ANGELO BADALAMENTI

KYRIE FOR THE MAGDALENE
from THE DA VINCI CODE

By RICHARD HARVEY

A LOVE BEFORE TIME

from the Motion Picture CROUCHING TIGER, HIDDEN DRAGON

Words and Music by KEVIN YI,
TAN DUN and JORGE CALANDRELLI

To Coda

D.S. al Coda

CODA

THE JOHN DUNBAR THEME

from DANCES WITH WOLVES

By JOHN BARRY

NEVERLAND –
PIANO VARIATIONS IN BLUE
from FINDING NEVERLAND

By A.P. KACZMAREK

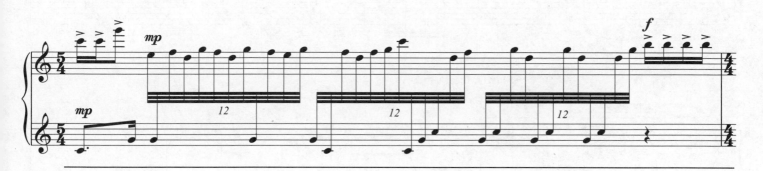

Slowly, in 2 (in time)

WE SHALL FIGHT
from DARKEST HOUR

By DARIO MARIANELLI

THE ENGLISH PATIENT
from THE ENGLISH PATIENT

Written by GABRIEL YARED

TUBULAR BELLS
Theme from THE EXORCIST

By MIKE OLDFIELD

To Coda ⊕

FAR AND AWAY

(Main Theme)

from the Universal Motion Picture FAR AND AWAY

Composed by JOHN WILLIAMS

THEME FROM "FATAL ATTRACTION"

from the Paramount Motion Picture FATAL ATTRACTION

Music by MAURICE JARRE

THE LANDING
from FIRST MAN

By JUSTIN HURWITZ

LOVE THEME FROM "FLASHDANCE"

from the Paramount Picture FLASHDANCE

Music by GIORGIO MORODER

FORREST GUMP – MAIN TITLE
(Feather Theme)
from the Paramount Motion Picture FORREST GUMP

Music by ALAN SILVESTRI

(lightly)

GOLDFINGER
from GOLDFINGER

Music by JOHN BARRY
Lyrics by LESLIE BRICUSSE
and ANTHONY NEWLEY

EARTH
from the Dreamworks film GLADIATOR

Written by HANS ZIMMER

113

THE GODFATHER
(Love Theme)
from the Paramount Picture THE GODFATHER

By NINO ROTA

THE GUNS OF NAVARONE
from THE GUNS OF NAVARONE

Words and Music by DIMITRI TIOMKIN
and PAUL WEBSTER

HEDWIG'S THEME
from the Motion Picture HARRY POTTER AND THE SORCERER'S STONE

By JOHN WILLIAMS

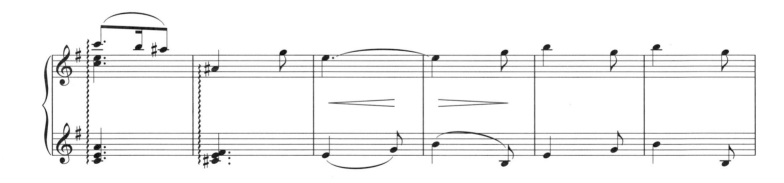

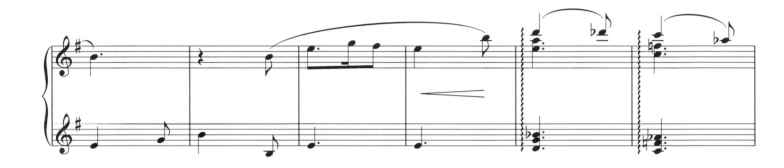

Brightly ($\dot{}$ = 80)

TEST DRIVE
from the Motion Picture HOW TO TRAIN YOUR DRAGON

By JOHN POWELL

Moderately

HEAVEN CAN WAIT
(Love Theme)
from the Paramount Motion Picture HEAVEN CAN WAIT

Music by DAVE GRUSIN

MAESTRO
from THE HOLIDAY

Music by HANS ZIMMER

Slowly, in 2

Play 4 times

mp

with pedal

mf

8va

(8va)

THE CLOCKS
from the Paramount Motion Picture HUGO

By HOWARD SHORE
Contains an excerpt from "Aubade Charmeuse"
by JEAN PEYRONNIN

Slightly faster (♩ = 120)

Moderately fast waltz, in 1 $(\licenseddotted = 66)$

rit.

Moderately (♩ = 120)

INCREDITS 2

from INCREDIBLES 2

Composed by
MICHAEL GIACCHINO

INDECENT PROPOSAL
(Main Theme)
from INDECENT PROPOSAL

By JOHN BARRY

THEME FROM "JURASSIC PARK"

from the Universal Motion Picture JURASSIC PARK

Composed by JOHN WILLIAMS

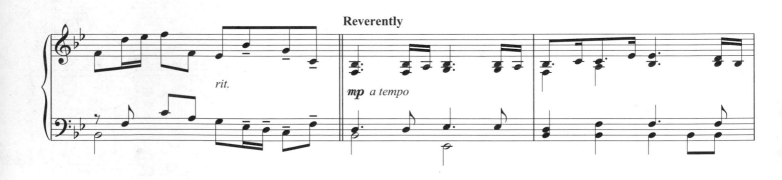

MIA & SEBASTIAN'S THEME
from LA LA LAND

Music by
JUSTIN HURWITZ

Moderately slow, expressively

LAST OF THE MOHICANS
(Main Theme)
from the Twentieth Century Fox Motion Picture THE LAST OF THE MOHICANS

By TREVOR JONES

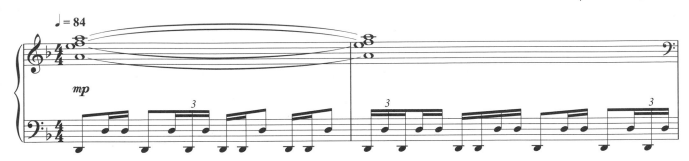

THE LUDLOWS
from TriStar Pictures' LEGENDS OF THE FALL

Composed by JAMES HORNER

CONCERNING HOBBITS

from THE LORD OF THE RINGS: THE FELLOWSHIP OF THE RING

By HOWARD SHORE

LOVE STORY
Theme from the Paramount Picture LOVE STORY

Music by FRANCIS LAI

GLASGOW LOVE THEME

from LOVE ACTUALLY

By CRAIG ARMSTRONG

Slowly, very freely

JESSICA'S THEME
(Breaking in the Colt)
from THE MAN FROM SNOWY RIVER

By BRUCE ROWLAND

CODA

THE MAN FROM SNOWY RIVER
(Main Title Theme)
from THE MAN FROM SNOWY RIVER

By BRUCE ROWLAND

AN AMERICAN SYMPHONY
from MR. HOLLAND'S OPUS

Composed by MICHAEL KAMEN

allargando

molto rall.

a tempo

THE CHAIRMAN'S WALTZ
from MEMOIRS OF A GEISHA

By JOHN WILLIAMS

SAYURI'S THEME
from MEMOIRS OF A GEISHA

By JOHN WILLIAMS

Moderately slow, in 2

pp

With pedal

GABRIEL'S OBOE
from the Motion Picture THE MISSION

Music by ENNIO MORRICONE

A PRAYER FOR PEACE

from MUNICH

Music by JOHN WILLIAMS

THE NAKED GUN
FROM THE FILES OF POLICE SQUAD!

Theme from the Paramount Picture THE NAKED GUN FROM THE FILES OF POLICE SQUAD

Music by IRA NEWBORN

NICHOLAS AND ALEXANDRA
Theme from NICHOLAS AND ALEXANDRA

By RICHARD RODNEY BENNETT

THE NUTCRACKER AND THE FOUR REALMS

from THE NUTCRACKER AND THE FOUR REALMS

Music by JAMES NEWTON HOWARD

THE HEART ASKS PLEASURE FIRST
from THE PIANO

By MICHAEL NYMAN

THE PINK PANTHER
from THE PINK PANTHER

By HENRY MANCINI

Moderately, mysterioso

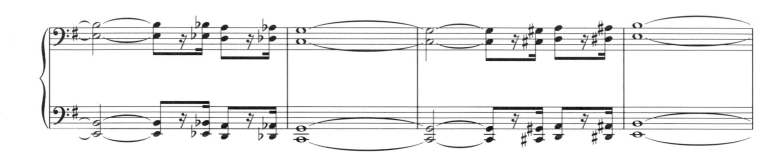

HE'S A PIRATE

from PIRATES OF THE CARIBBEAN: THE CURSE OF THE BLACK PEARL

Written by HANS ZIMMER,
KLAUS BADELT and GEOFF ZANELLI

THE PRESSES ROLL
from THE POST

By JOHN WILLIAMS

Moderately fast

molto rit.

THE PROMISE
(I'll Never Say Goodbye)
Theme from the Universal Motion Picture THE PROMISE

Words by ALAN and MARILYN BERGMAN
Music by DAVID SHIRE

DAWN
from PRIDE & PREJUDICE

By DARIO MARIANELLI

Moderately fast, with motion

Slightly slower

GEORGIANA
from PRIDE & PREJUDICE

By DARIO MARIANELLI

Moderately fast, in 4

RATATOUILLE MAIN THEME
from RATATOUILLE

Music by MICHAEL GIACCHINO

GALE'S THEME

(Main Title)
from THE RIVER WILD

By JERRY GOLDSMITH

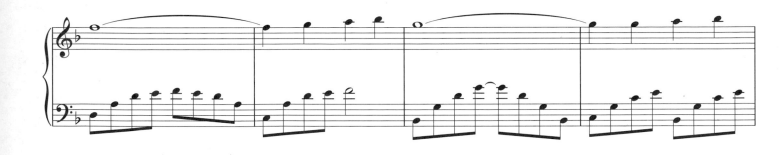

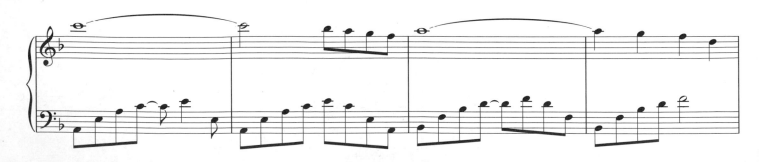

HYMN TO THE FALLEN

from the Paramount and DreamWorks Motion Picture SAVING PRIVATE RYAN

Music by JOHN WILLIAMS

Slightly faster

mf

cresc.

f

3

ROAD TO PERDITION
from the Motion Picture ROAD TO PERDITION

By THOMAS NEWMAN

THEME FROM "SABRINA"
from the Paramount Motion Picture SABRINA

By JOHN WILLIAMS

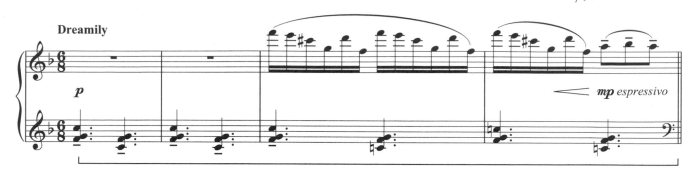

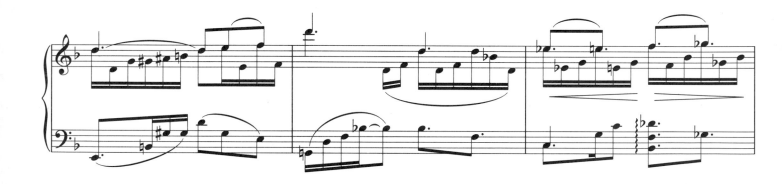

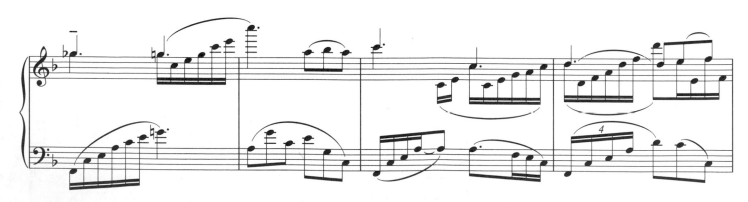

THEME FROM "SCHINDLER'S LIST"

from the Universal Motion Picture SCHINDLER'S LIST

Music by JOHN WILLIAMS

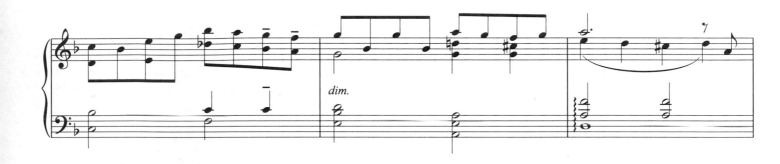

MY FATHER'S FAVORITE
from SENSE AND SENSIBILITY

By PATRICK DOYLE

THE SHAPE OF WATER

from THE SHAPE OF WATER

By ALEXANDRE DESPLAT

THE ADVENTURES OF HAN

from SOLO: A STAR WARS STORY

Composed by
JOHN WILLIAMS

SOMEWHERE IN TIME

from SOMEWHERE IN TIME

Music by JOHN BARRY

SPARTACUS – LOVE THEME

from the Universal-International Picture Release SPARTACUS

By ALEX NORTH

STAR WARS
(Main Theme)
from STAR WARS: A NEW HOPE

Music by JOHN WILLIAMS

simile

(Theme From)
A SUMMER PLACE

from A SUMMER PLACE

Words by MACK DISCANT
Music by MAX STEINER

THEME FROM SUMMER OF '42
(The Summer Knows)
from SUMMER OF '42

Music by MICHEL LEGRAND

Slowly

FORCES OF ATTRACTION
from THE THEORY OF EVERYTHING

By JÓHANN JÓHANNSSON
Arranged by Anthony Weeden

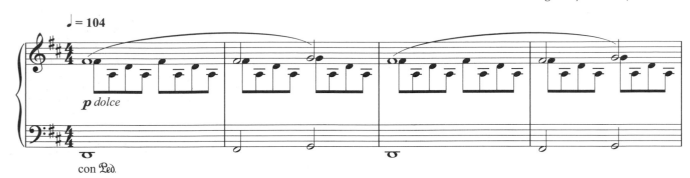

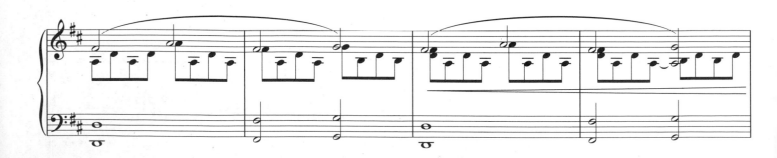

THE WINDMILLS OF YOUR MIND

Theme from THE THOMAS CROWN AFFAIR

Words by ALAN and MARILYN BERGMAN
Music by MICHEL LEGRAND

IT MIGHT BE YOU
Theme from TOOTSIE

Words by ALAN and MARILYN BERGMAN
Music by DAVE GRUSIN

BELLA'S LULLABY

from the Summit Entertainment film TWILIGHT

By CARTER BURWELL

JACOB'S THEME

from the Summit Entertainment film THE TWILIGHT SAGA: ECLIPSE

Composed by HOWARD SHORE

Rubato

REMEMBERING EMILIE, AND FINALE

from the Motion Picture WAR HORSE

Composed by
JOHN WILLIAMS

Moderately, expressively

p

With pedal

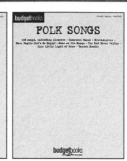

THE BEST EVER

COLLECTION
ARRANGED FOR PIANO, VOICE AND GUITAR

100 of the Most Beautiful Piano Solos Ever
100 songs
00102787 ....$27.50

150 of the Most Beautiful Songs Ever
150 ballads
00360735 ....$27.00

More of the Best Acoustic Rock Songs Ever
69 tunes
00311738 ....$19.95

Best Acoustic Rock Songs Ever
65 acoustic hits
00310984 ....$22.99

Best Big Band Songs Ever
66 favorites
00286933 ....$19.99

Best Blues Songs Ever
73 blues tunes
00312874 ....$19.99

Best Broadway Songs Ever
83 songs
00309155 ....$24.99

More of the Best Broadway Songs Ever
82 songs
00311501 ....$22.95

Best Children's Songs Ever
101 songs
00159272 ....$19.99

Best Christmas Songs Ever
69 holiday favorites
00359130 ....$27.50

Best Classic Rock Songs Ever
64 hits
00289313 ....$24.99

Best Classical Music Ever
86 classical favorites
00310674 (Piano Solo) $19.95

The Best Country Rock Songs Ever
52 hits
00118881 ....$19.99

Best Country Songs Ever
78 classic country hits
00359135 ....$19.99

Best Disco Songs Ever
50 songs
00312565 ....$19.99

Best Early Rock 'n' Roll Songs Ever
74 songs
00310816 ....$19.95

Best Easy Listening Songs Ever
75 mellow favorites
00359193 ....$22.99

Best Folk/Pop Songs Ever
66 hits
00138299 ....$19.99

Best Gospel Songs Ever
80 gospel songs
00310503 ....$19.99

Best Hymns Ever
118 hymns
00310774 ....$18.99

Best Jazz Piano Solos Ever
80 songs
00312079 ....$19.99

Best Jazz Standards Ever
77 jazz hits
00311641 ....$19.95

Best Latin Songs Ever
67 songs
00310355 ....$19.99

Best Love Songs Ever
62 favorite love songs
00359198 ....$19.99

Best Movie Songs Ever
71 songs
00310063 ....$19.99

Best Movie Soundtrack Songs Ever
70 songs
00146161 ....$19.99

Best Pop/Rock Songs Ever
50 classics
00138279 ....$19.99

Best Praise & Worship Songs Ever
80 all-time favorites
00311057 ....$22.99

Best R&B Songs Ever
66 songs
00310184 ....$19.95

Best Rock Songs Ever
63 songs
00490424 ....$18.95

Best Songs Ever
71 must-own classics
00265721 ....$24.99

Best Soul Songs Ever
70 hits
00311427 ....$19.95

Best Standards Ever, Vol. 1 (A-L)
72 beautiful ballads
00359231 ....$17.95

Best Standards Ever, Vol. 2 (M-Z)
73 songs
00359232 ....$17.99

Best Wedding Songs Ever
70 songs
00290985 ....$19.99

HAL•LEONARD®
Visit us online
for complete songlists at
www.halleonard.com

THE NEW DECADE SERIES

Books with Online Audio • Arranged for Piano, Voice, and Guitar

The New Decade Series features collections of iconic songs from each decade with great backing tracks so you can play them and sound like a pro. You access the tracks online for streaming or download. **See complete song listings online at www.halleonard.com**

SONGS OF THE 1920s
Ain't Misbehavin' • Baby Face • California, Here I Come • Fascinating Rhythm • I Wanna Be Loved by You • It Had to Be You • Mack the Knife • Ol' Man River • Puttin' on the Ritz • Rhapsody in Blue • Someone to Watch over Me • Tea for Two • Who's Sorry Now • and more.
00137576 P/V/G.....................................$24.99

SONGS OF THE 1930s
As Time Goes By • Blue Moon • Cheek to Cheek • Embraceable You • A Fine Romance • Georgia on My Mind • I Only Have Eyes for You • The Lady Is a Tramp • On the Sunny Side of the Street • Over the Rainbow • Pennies from Heaven • Stormy Weather (Keeps Rainin' All the Time) • The Way You Look Tonight • and more.
00137579 P/V/G.....................................$24.99

SONGS OF THE 1940s
At Last • Boogie Woogie Bugle Boy • Don't Get Around Much Anymore • God Bless' the Child • How High the Moon • It Could Happen to You • La Vie En Rose (Take Me to Your Heart Again) • Route 66 • Sentimental Journey • The Trolley Song • You'd Be So Nice to Come Home To • Zip-A-Dee-Doo-Dah • and more.
00137582 P/V/G.....................................$24.99

SONGS OF THE 1950s
Ain't That a Shame • Be-Bop-A-Lula • Chantilly Lace • Earth Angel • Fever • Great Balls of Fire • Love Me Tender • Mona Lisa • Peggy Sue • Que Sera, Sera (Whatever Will Be, Will Be) • Rock Around the Clock • Sixteen Tons • A Teenager in Love • That'll Be the Day • Unchained Melody • Volare • You Send Me • Your Cheatin' Heart • and more.
00137595 P/V/G.....................................$24.99

SONGS OF THE 1960s
All You Need Is Love • Beyond the Sea • Born to Be Wild • California Girls • Dancing in the Street • Happy Together • King of the Road • Leaving on a Jet Plane • Louie, Louie • My Generation • Oh, Pretty Woman • Sunshine of Your Love • Under the Boardwalk • You Really Got Me • and more.
00137596 P/V/G.....................................$24.99

SONGS OF THE 1970s
ABC • Bridge over Troubled Water • Cat's in the Cradle • Dancing Queen • Free Bird • Goodbye Yellow Brick Road • Hotel California • I Will Survive • Joy to the World • Killing Me Softly with His Song • Layla • Let It Be • Piano Man • The Rainbow Connection • Stairway to Heaven • The Way We Were • Your Song • and more.
00137599 P/V/G.....................................$27.99

SONGS OF THE 1980s
Addicted to Love • Beat It • Careless Whisper • Come on Eileen • Don't Stop Believin' • Every Rose Has Its Thorn • Footloose • I Just Called to Say I Love You • Jessie's Girl • Livin' on a Prayer • Saving All My Love for You • Take on Me • Up Where We Belong • The Wind Beneath My Wings • and more.
00137600 P/V/G.....................................$27.99

SONGS OF THE 1990s
Angel • Black Velvet • Can You Feel the Love Tonight • (Everything I Do) I Do It for You • Friends in Low Places • Hero • I Will Always Love You • More Than Words • My Heart Will Go On (Love Theme from 'Titanic') • Smells like Teen Spirit • Under the Bridge • Vision of Love • Wonderwall • and more.
00137601 P/V/G.....................................$27.99

SONGS OF THE 2000s
Bad Day • Beautiful • Before He Cheats • Chasing Cars • Chasing Pavements • Drops of Jupiter (Tell Me) • Fireflies • Hey There Delilah • How to Save a Life • I Gotta Feeling • I'm Yours • Just Dance • Love Story • 100 Years • Rehab • Unwritten • You Raise Me Up • and more.
00137608 P/V/G.....................................$27.99

SONGS OF THE 2010s
All About That Bass • All of Me • Brave • Empire State of Mind • Get Lucky • Happy • Hey, Soul Sister • I Knew You Were Trouble • Just the Way You Are • Need You Now • Pompeii • Radioactive • Rolling in the Deep • Shake It Off • Shut up and Dance • Stay with Me • Take Me to Church • Thinking Out Loud • Uptown Funk • and many more.
00151836 P/V/G.....................................$27.99

HAL•LEONARD®

halleonard.com
Prices, content, and availability subject to change without notice.